BAREFOOT BOOKS

The barefoot child symbolizes the human being whose natural integrity and capacity for action are unimpaired. In this spirit, Barefoot Books publishes new and traditional myths, legends, and fairy tales whose themes demonstrate the pitfalls and dangers that surround our passage through life; the qualities that are needed to face and overcome these dangers; and the equal importance of action and reflection in doing so. Our intention is to present stories from a wide range of cultures in such a way as to delight and inspire readers of all ages while honoring the tradition from which the story has been inherited.

THE MYTH OF ISIS AND OSIRIS

☥

R E T O L D   B Y

J U L E S   C A S H F O R D

BAREFOOT BOOKS

BOSTON & BATH

BAREFOOT BOOKS
the children's books imprint of
Shambhala Publications, Inc.
Horticultural Hall
300 Massachusetts Avenue
Boston, Massachusetts 02115

FOREWORD

The story of Isis and Osiris was the great myth of ancient Egypt for over three thousand years – from before 3000 BC to the second century AD. Story-telling is the oldest art in the world, and this story is one of the oldest to come down to us, written two thousand years before Homer wrote down the tales of the Trojan War.

Myths and stories, as also dreams, images, and symbols, always hold much more than any possible interpretation of them, and are often best left alone to speak for themselves in their own way. Our myths are the sacred stories through which we try to make sense of the world we live in. They dramatize the essential questions that children in all ages have asked: How did we get here? Who made the world? Why do we suffer? What is death? How should we live?

The ancient Egyptians explored these questions in the context of the overwhelming reality of their daily lives: the annual rising and falling of the River Nile, on which their life depended. The land of Egypt is re-created every year by this river which flows from south to north, from the Equator to the Mediterranean. Life was – and still is – contained in a narrow valley on either side of the river. Beyond this lies desert, a barren land of sand and rock with no water and no shade from the burning sun.

Every year it seemed to the ancient Egyptians as if the Nile died – and was reborn. Around the summer solstice, in mid-June, the Nile shrank as though it would disappear completely, but slowly it began to swell until it burst its banks and flooded over the shriveled land. Only in autumn did the waters recede, leaving the fields ready for seeding in November. It was not possible to regulate the inundation: too great a flood and the irrigation canals collapsed; too little, and the people went hungry.

The building of the Aswan dam in the 1960s, designed to control the flow of water throughout the year, consigned to history thousands of years of unchanged agricultural practice. But if we imagine ourselves back in ancient Egypt, we can perhaps see how this yearly event was experienced as a cosmic drama in which all the forces of the universe were engaged.

As in all our own dreams and imaginings, myths personify: feelings become persons; different kinds of feelings, as people, talk to each other; where feelings conflict, people take sides, quarrel and injure each other; when a new level of feeling emerges from such a conflict, a child is born. So it is that the joy of life becomes Osiris and the fear of death becomes Seth; the love which transforms bad into good becomes Isis and the longing to help becomes Nephthys. And so, more widely, Osiris becomes the life-force of Nature which dies and is reborn, or is killed and brought back to life again. Isis becomes the redemptive force of love in Nature which brings forth new life out of old, and Horus becomes the new form in which the old life is reenacted – so nothing is lost.

When the Nile fell and the plants withered, when the corn was threshed by the ass, and even when the moon started to wane, the Egyptians said that Seth was killing Osiris. It was when the moon was full that Seth discovered the casket in the reeds, and it was into fourteen pieces that he dismembered the body of Osiris – the exact number of days of the waning moon when it 'loses' its light to the darkness. When the Nile began to rise again, they said it was watered by the tears of Isis as she searched for her husband. When it overflowed, they said that Isis had found Osiris. The water covering the land resembled the primeval waters, the source of creation. Then, when the shoots nudged up out of the earth, they said that Osiris lived again and that all life was reborn as it was in the first time.

As children, we are still in touch with this symbolic imagination. The darkness can be filled with monsters, the garden with flower fairies, the air with magical voices; there can be anything under the bed or behind the closed door.

In this world animals and birds speak to us, beckon us to follow them, show us what to do. The Egyptians listened to their animals and birds because, unlike humans, these creatures seemed to have been there always, and to know the way things were in the very beginning. The ibis, who has a long curved beak which he plunges deep into the water, can sift out tiny insects and fish from the thick dense mud. He can also fly great distances. So Thoth, the Wise, has the head of an ibis and teaches us discrimination and insight. He appears in the story when that quality is needed; when, for instance, another way of thinking is required to resolve the conflict between Horus and Seth. The long-nosed jackal, who hunts at night, can find pieces of food he has buried beneath the earth and knows exactly when to dig them up again before they decay. He, as it were, saves them from falling out of the life-cycle of animals; he transforms them. So Anubis, who has the head, and sometimes the whole body, of a jackal, helps Isis to find the dismembered body of Osiris and to put it together again.

To play with the image, Anubis teaches us that when we have lost or forgotten something, we need to grow a long nose and prick up our ears! We may think of a kite as just a scavenging bird, but this is what Isis becomes when she brings Osiris back to life and conceives Horus from him, scavenging life from death. Horus as a hawk is undeviating, sudden and swift; he tells us that anything new demands the intensity of this bird to break free from the structures of the old. In this he resembles the Sun, Ra, who has to overcome the Serpent of Darkness each night, and often takes the form of a falcon. Especially in summer, the scorching Egyptian sun must have seemed to pierce through the skies like a bird of prey.

The myth as a whole describes the origin of the universe (in the Waters of Life which contain all things) and of the elements necessary to life (air and moisture) and of how our world is structured (into heaven and earth and the space between). Then it explores the underlying reality beneath what we see – the principles of what we might call Nature, including human nature – through the story of Isis and Osiris, Seth and Nephthys. This myth dramatizes the dialogue of order and disorder, good and evil, life and death. In the course of the story an equilibrium is achieved: the rhythms of the year and, it may be, of life itself become intelligible.

Every year, after the inundation, people would come from all over Egypt to a little town beside the Nile called Abydos, in order to celebrate the Mysteries of Osiris, where the drama of his life, death, and rebirth was ritually enacted. The Egyptian New Year began at the moment when the pillar of Osiris – the Djed – pillar, crafted in wood with four branches (once perhaps a pole with four sheaves of corn tied across it) – was raised from the ground to stand stable and upright as an image of the reawakening of Osiris and, through him, the resurgence of all life.

The appeal of the myth of Isis and Osiris lay in the fact that people could identify with them as sharing the fate of human beings, yet they also transcended the limitations of the human condition. Isis lost her husband but found him and revived him. She brought her child up alone, overcame his sicknesses, and he grew up to take his father's place. When the ancient Egyptians lost their loved ones, they mourned like Isis, and they imagined that when they died they became like Osiris, continuing to live in another realm as he did. So the Egyptians also saw in the death and revival of Osiris an analogy for human life after death. They constructed a vivid picture of this existence, when the person's life would be evaluated by weighing the heart against a feather – the Feather of Truth. A "light" heart got through, so to speak, and then the person would be led into the presence of Osiris. He or she would meet his or her soul, in the image of a beautiful blue phoenix, shown opposite with the crown of Osiris, indicating that the soul of the deceased and the soul of Osiris have become one.

Jules Cashford

A NOTE ON THE TEXT

☥

The original, ancient Egyptian, text of the myth of Isis and Osiris does not exist in a complete form, but it is possible to reconstruct it from many different sources: hieroglyphic writings on the walls of pyramids and the insides of coffins; books of papyrus laid in tombs; hymns and poems copied by scribes; and, above all, the magnificent paintings on the walls of the great valley tombs of Upper Egypt, carved deep into the desert rock and covered over by sand for thousands of years.

The Greek writer Plutarch traveled to Egypt in the first century AD and wrote down his version of the myth after talking to the Egyptian people and hearing about the great festival held every year at Abydos following the inundation of the Nile. His story remained for a long time the only written version that people knew since Egyptian hieroglyphic writing could not be deciphered until 1822.

In 1799, in a place called Rosetta, Napoleon's soldiers found a large stone in the sand – now kept in the British Museum as the "Rosetta Stone" – which had the same passage inscribed upon it in three different languages: Greek, Egyptian hieroglyphs, and demotic, nonpictorial hieroglyphs. By matching the Greek words with the other two languages, scholars were able to break the "code" and to translate all manner of ancient Egyptian inscriptions. It became clear that Plutarch's story coincided closely with the other stories from the original Egyptian culture, even though they were incomplete.

THE MYTH OF ISIS AND OSIRIS

☥

In the beginning were the Waters of Life and the Waters of Life were everywhere and the name of the Waters was Nun. In them was everything that was to come. Atum, "the One," rested motionless in the waters and longed for the world to come into being. Out of this longing were born a son, Shu, and a daughter, Tefnut. Shu was Air and Tefnut was Moisture. For a long time they lay in the loving embrace of Atum their father and Atum their mother. Then they vanished in the dark waters and were lost. So the Eye of Atum separated from Atum and went out into the darkness to look for them, and after many ages it found them and brought them back.

Atum kissed them and gave them new names: Shu became Life and Tefnut became Order.

Then Atum rose from the waters as the First Hill and shone from the waters as the First Light. Now Atum became Atum-Ra: Ra was the visible face of Atum the Sun. Atum was the invisible whole.

Shu and Tefnut gave birth to a son, Geb, and a daughter, Nut. Geb was Earth and Nut was Sky. But Sky held Earth so close that there was no space between them. So Shu lifted up Sky, his daughter Nut, and held her high above him in an arch until only the tips of her fingers and the tips of her toes touched Earth, Geb, his son.

In the evening Nut swallowed the Sun through her mouth and the world outside became dark. Then the stars came forth from Nut and moved across her body, sparkling in the night. At dawn Nut gave birth to the Sun, like a mother gives birth to her baby.

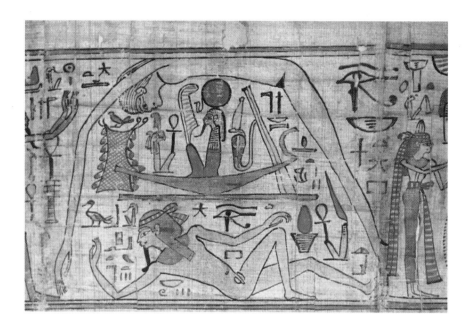

Nut and Geb gave birth to two sons, Osiris and Seth, and two daughters, Isis and Nephthys.

Geb gave Osiris the rich soil, the waving corn and the clustering vines, the seeds, the flowers and the fruit. Osiris loved black Nile, the river who winds like a serpent through the land called Egypt, flowing over the banks to make the fields fertile and the crops grow tall. Sometimes he took the form of a bull.

Nut gave Isis rain and dew and all the wet and moist places of the earth. Without Isis no seed could sprout and no plant could grow. She was there when the moon was full of light, when the dawn came, when the Dog Star, Sothis, rose on the eastern horizon just before the Nile overflowed. Her breath was the breath of life and her milk nourished all the creatures on earth. Sometimes she took the form of a cow or a star or a tree.

Seth, the younger brother, had hair as red as the desert where the Sun burned all day, scorching the ground so nothing could grow. He sent the harsh storm winds which blew the hot dry sands out of the desert across the green fields. He loved the salt sea which scattered the waters of the Nile, and the darkness

which swallowed up the Sun each night. Sometimes he took the form of a crocodile or a hippopotamus or an ass.

Nephthys, the younger sister, belonged to the darkness as her sister Isis belonged to the light. Nephthys loved the waning and dark moon while Isis loved the new and full moon. The morning star was the star of Isis and the evening star was the star of Nephthys. The two sisters were so close they were like one person with different names: Isis was the visible one and Nephthys was the invisible one.

When they grew up Isis married Osiris and Nephthys married Seth.

One day Atum wept tears of joy, and from the tears came all the people of the world.

Osiris taught the people the art of civilization. He showed them how to gather the fruit from the trees and how to plough the fields and plant wheat and barley which they could make into bread. He gave them laws to bring order to their lives, and he inspired them to honor the source of life and the principles of justice in the universe. He journeyed over the whole earth, bringing civilization to all nations, charming them with music and song. While

he was away Isis ruled peacefully, watching over the land.

When Osiris returned home everyone was happy – except his brother Seth. Seth rebelled against order and justice. His heart was heavy with his desire to take the place of Osiris. So he got together seventy-two conspirators and whispered to them his wicked plot. Stealthily, he measured the body of Osiris and made a magnificent

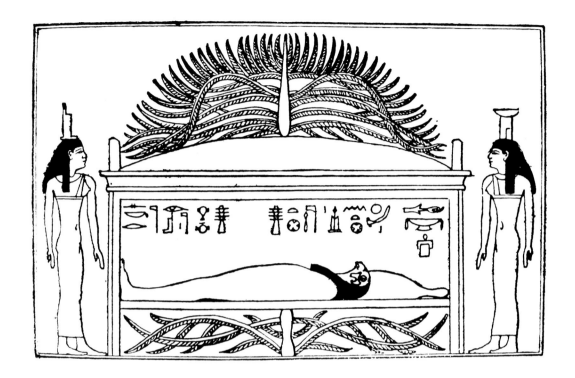

chest of the same size, with brightly colored pictures painted all round it. Then they held a party.

In the banqueting hall everyone was drinking and eating and laughing and having a good time. At the height of the feast Seth had the chest brought into the room; all the people were amazed. He waited his moment and said:

'Whoever shall lie down in this chest and fit it exactly, that person shall have it for himself. This I promise.'

They all tried in turn, but it fitted none of them. Last of all Osiris lay down in the chest. It fitted him perfectly.

Immediately the conspirators rushed toward the chest and slammed down the lid. They hammered in long nails and sealed it with lead. Then they threw it into the Nile and the river swept it out to sea.

Isis was heart-broken. She cut off a braid of her hair and put on clothes of mourning. Then she set out to search for her husband. It was the children who

told her where the casket was. They were playing by the sea when they saw it floating by. Now Isis knew where to look.

She learned that the waves had gently set down the casket on the shore at Byblos in Phoenicia. A tamarisk tree had grown up around it, enclosing the casket in its trunk, until it was completely hidden. So beautiful was the tree that the king of Byblos had it cut down and made into a pillar at his palace.

Isis came to Byblos in disguise and sat down beside a spring. When the servants of the queen came to fetch water, she smiled at them and began to plait their hair, breathing sweetly over them. The queen smelt the fragrance on their hair and asked them whom they had met. When they told her she sent for Isis and begged her to nurse her baby boy.

Isis gave the infant her finger to suck instead of her breast, and at night she placed him in a fire to burn away all that was mortal in him. While he was sleeping in the fire she would turn herself into a swallow and fly around the pillar, singing mournfully. But one night the queen peeped into the room and saw her little son lying in the flames and screamed.

Now Isis revealed who she was and all in the palace were astonished. She asked for the pillar to be cut down and given to her. She stripped away the bark and, finding the casket inside, she fell upon it and wept. Then she commanded that the casket be lifted on to a boat, and she sailed out to sea to bring it home. When she was sure no one could see her, she opened it and saw her dear love lying as though asleep, and kissed him. Suddenly she became a kite – a huge bird with great strong wings – and with the beating of her wings she created a mighty wind which gave him back the Breath of Life. Then she conceived her son, Horus, from him.

When she landed she concealed the casket among the tall reeds of the marshes in the Delta, and went away secretly to give birth to Horus.

But one night, when the moon was full, Seth was hunting wild boar and saw the casket and recognized it. He ripped off the lid and in a furious rage he tore the poor body of Osiris into fourteen pieces and scattered them all over Egypt.

When Isis heard this, she paddled over the swamps in a little boat looking for the fragments of Osiris to put them back together again and make him whole. The crocodiles felt so sorry for her they did not tip over her boat as they often did to others but let her pass between them. On land her sister Nephthys helped her, and so did Nephthys' own son, Anubis, who was like a jackal and had a very good nose for finding things.

After much searching they found all the parts of Osiris except his phallus which had been swallowed by a fish. But Isis made a model of the missing part and then she reassembled all the pieces of the body of Osiris until he looked just as he had done before.

Then, with the help of Anubis, she performed a special ritual over him and he came back to life. So Osiris went to rule the Underworld as he had once ruled the Earth. Every night Ra, the Sun, comes to wake him up just at the time when everyone else has fallen fast asleep.

After that Isis hurried back to Horus in the marshes and brought him up in secret and they had many adventures together.

Once, when she was away finding food for them both, he was bitten by a scorpion and got very hot and feverish. But she heard him calling from a long way off and came back and healed him with a magic spell which Thoth, the Wise One, had given her. Seth was always looking for them but the reeds hid them and he could not find them.

One day Isis realized that Horus had grown up into a man. Sometimes he took the form of a hawk and looked very fierce. Then he looked like Ra, the Sun, who often appeared as a soaring falcon.

'I shall go and right the great wrong that was done to my father,' he said. 'I shall find Seth.'

When Horus found Seth he challenged him to combat. They wrestled with each other for three days and three nights – just as long as the moon was dark – but neither of them could win. Then Thoth, who had the head of an ibis and knew the difference between good and bad, came between them. He told them that force could not make a wrong right. So Isis and Horus went and stood before the Court of the Law and told their story and appealed for justice.

The Court called for Seth to give his side of the story, which he did, but no one believed his excuses.

The verdict was given:

'Seth must carry the boat of the Sun as it crosses the sky. He must overcome the Serpent of Darkness who tries to capture the Sun each night. He must carry the boat of Osiris when he journeys up and down the Nile.'

This was the judgment of Atum-Ra. Seth obeyed.

Now Thoth placed a double crown on the head of Horus. It was red and white and it gleamed. Horus climbed the steps to the throne of his father and took his place. He was now King of the Upperworld as Osiris was King of the Underworld. Thoth also offered the Breath of Life to Osiris.

Then Horus went down to the Underworld to tell his father that justice had been done. He called out to him:

'Rise, Osiris!

You went away, but now you have returned.

Rise, Osiris!

You were asleep, but now you are awake.

Rise Osiris! You died, but now you live again.'

He gave him a gift, the Eye of Eternity, which would always protect him. Now Osiris sits on his throne in the Hall of Truth. He greets the souls of the dead after their hearts have been weighed against the Feather of Truth. If their

hearts are as light as the feather, he welcomes them to his world.

When Horus came back from the Underworld, he embraced his mother Isis and together they raised up a statue to Osiris as a sign of his reawakening and of their happiness. It was a pillar made from a tree, and was called the Djed-pillar. They hung so many garlands upon it that it looked as though it was blossoming with leaves.

Then there were celebrations all over Egypt. The Nile burst his banks for joy and the thick black waters spread over the land, making it rich and soft. Soon seeds began to shoot and plants began to grow. The New Year had begun.

So every year, forever afterward, the people remembered the death of Osiris, when the Nile dried up and the plants withered. And when the Nile rose and overflowed and the land was covered in flowers, the people remembered how Osiris rose again from the dead and is always with us.

PICTURE ACKNOWLEDGMENTS

Figure 1.   Gold pectoral in the form of winged Isis: *c.* 710-663 BC. Kushite tomb of King Amarinataki-lebte, Nuri, Sudan. (Museum of Fine Arts, Boston, Mass., Harvard University, MFA Expedition)

Figure 2.   The man Anhurkhawl meeting his Soul with the crown of Osiris: *c.* 1190-1085 BC. Tomb of Anhurkhawl, Deir el-Medina, Thebes. (Hirmer Fotoarchiv, Munich)

Figure 3.   The Eye of Atum, guarded by the vulture and cobra goddesses of Upper and Lower Egypt: *c.* 1350 BC. Jewel of Tutankhamun, Tomb of Tutankhamun (Cairo Museum). (Photograph from Lucie Lamy, *Egyptian Mysteries: New Light on Ancient Knowledge*, Thames & Hudson, London, 1981, p. 44)

Figure 4.   Shu, Air, separating Nut, Sky, from Geb, Earth. *c.* 1000 BC. Book of the Dead of Nespakashouti (Musée du Louvre, Réunions des Musées nationaux)

Figure 5.   Isis as the Tree of Life offering milk to human beings: *c.* 1479-1425 BC. Tomb of Tuthmosis III, Valley of the Kings, Thebes. (Photograph from Andreas Brodbeck in Erik Hornung, *Valley of the Kings: Horizon of Eternity*, Timken Publishers, New York, 1990, p. 63)

Figure 6.   Isis on her golden throne holding the Ring of Eternity: *c.* 1427-1401 BC Sarcophagus of Amenhotep II, Valley of the Kings, Thebes. (Hirmer Fotoarchiv, Munich)

Figure 7.   Osiris in his casket in the tamarisk tree, watched over by Isis and Nephthys: bas-relief, *c.* first century BC. Temple of Denderah. (Drawing by Robin Baring after E. A. Wallis Budge, *Osiris and the Egyptian Resurrection*, Dover Publications, New York, 1973, vol. 1, p. 5)

Figure 8. Isis holding a rattle and a necklace. On the right, Osiris – holding a crook and flail and a long sceptre – receives incense: *c.* 1300 BC. Temple of Seti I, Abydos. (Hirmer Fotoarchiv, Munich)

Figure 9. Isis suckling the infant Horus on her lap: bronze statue, *c.* 2040-1700 BC. (Staatliche Museen zu Berlin – Preubischer Kulturbesitz Egyptisches Museum und Papyrussammlung)

Figure 10. Anubis on a shrine: *c.* 1350 BC. Tomb of Tutankhamun, Valley of the Kings, Thebes. (Hirmer Fotoarchiv, Munich)

Figure 11. Isis suckling Horus in the reeds of the marshes in the Delta. (Drawing by Lyn Constable-Maxwell after R. T. Rundle Clark, *Myth and Symbol in Ancient Egypt*, Thames & Hudson, London, 1978, p. 107)

Figure 12. Seth, with an ass's head, on the boat of Ra, the Sun, in the form of a falcon, spearing the Serpent of Darkness: *c.* 1085-950 BC. The Book of the Dead of Lady Cheritwebeshet (Cairo Museum). (Photograph from Hannelore Kishkewitz, *Egyptian Art: Drawings and Paintings*, Hamlyn, London, 1989, plate 50)

Figure 13. Thoth offering the Breath of Life to Seti I as Osiris: *c.* 1300 BC. Temple of Seti I, Abydos. (Hirmer Fotoarchiv, Munich)

Figure 14. Osiris with two Eyes of Eternity: *c.* 1190-1085 BC. Tomb of Sennejem, Deir el-Medina, Thebes. (Hirmer Fotoarchiv, Munich)

Figure 15. The Weighing of the Soul against the Feather of Truth: *c.* 1310 BC. The Book of the Dead of Hunefer. (British Museum)

Figure 16. Osiris in the Hall of Truth with Isis and Nephthys behind him: *c.* 1310 BC. The Book of the Dead of Hunefer. (British Museum)

Figure 17. The Sun in the form of a falcon rising from the Djed-pillar, watched over by Isis and Nephthys, and greeted by baboons: *c.* 1310 BC. The Book of the Dead of Hunefer. (British Museum)